The Little Servant Girl

Retold by Felicity Henderson

Illustrations by Toni Goffe

D0645184

A LION BOOK
Oxford · Batavia · Sydney

Naaman and his wife were very glad to have such a helpful, happy servant.

One day the little servant girl saw Naaman's wife crying.

"What's the matter?" she asked.

"Oh dear," said Naaman's wife. "Whatever shall we do? Naaman is rich and famous but..." She burst into tears.

Naaman was upset too. He was ill.
There was something wrong with his
skin. He was covered with white spots.
Nothing would make them go away.

He saw all the doctors in the land. He
tried all the ointments and creams they
gave him. He said spells and ate special
food.

But still the spots got worse.

When people saw him they ran away.
"We don't want to catch your spots,"
they said.

The King told him he could not lead
the army any more.

Naaman was desperate. "Whatever
shall I do?" he cried.

All this time the little servant girl had been thinking of a plan.

"Please sir," she said. "There's someone who could help. His name is Elisha. He's a man of God in Israel. He could ask our God to make you well."

Straight away Naaman went to the King and asked if he might go to Israel.

"Go," said the King. "And take this letter, and some presents, and gold and silver."

So Naaman began his long journey.

At last he arrived at the house of Elisha the prophet, a man of God.

Elisha did not ask Naaman into his house.

Instead a servant came out with a message: "Go and wash yourself seven times in the River Jordan."

Naaman was furious.

"I've come all this way, and you tell me to wash in your river seven times. I've got better rivers at home!" he yelled.

But his men persuaded him to do as the man of God said.

One, two, three, four, five, six, seven!

On the seventh time Naaman came out of the river, the spots had disappeared!

"I'm better!" he shouted, and began to dance around.

He rushed off to Elisha to pay him.

"You don't have to pay me," said
Elisha. "But thank God who has made
you well."

Naaman was amazed. The God of
Israel had healed him.

God loved even the enemies of his
people.

The little servant girl couldn't wait for
Naaman to come home.

The little servant girl had to work hard. There was a lot of cooking and cleaning to do.

Sometimes she was sad because she missed her home. But she knew that God cared for her and was looking after her. When she remembered this she would feel happy again and would sing as she did her work.

Sometimes Naaman's soldiers would take prisoners after a battle. One day they captured a little Israelite girl.

Naaman took her to his house to work as a servant for his family.

Long ago, in a far-off land, the Syrians and Israelites and were fighting a war.

One of the Syrian soldiers was called Naaman. He was a great general who had won many battles and was very famous.

"You were right," said Naaman. "God does look after people."

"I'm so happy," said the little servant girl. "God loves us all and cares for everyone who asks him to." And she danced and clapped her hands for joy.

Text copyright © 1991 Lion Publishing
Illustrations copyright © 1991 Toni Goffe

Published by
Lion Publishing plc
Sandy Lane West, Oxford, England
ISBN 0 7459 2126 4
Lion Publishing Corporation
1705 Hubbard Avenue, Batavia, Illinois 60510, USA
ISBN 0 7459 2126 4
Albatross Books Pty Ltd
PO Box 320, Sutherland, NSW 2232, Australia
ISBN 0 7324 0476 2

First edition 1991

All rights reserved

Printed and bound in Singapore